ONCE AROUND THE SUN
JOBY TALBOT
FOR SOLO PIANO

CHESTER MUSIC

When I'd recovered from the initial excitement of being asked to be Classic FM's first ever composer in residence, the sheer scale of the challenge ahead sank in. I was asked to write and record twelve pieces in as many months; each new piece to be broadcast on Classic FM more or less as soon as I finished it. A month, I soon discovered, is a surprisingly short space of time – just long enough, in fact, to get yourself well and truly tied up in knots with an enormous deadline looming! But despite the odd panic, I managed not to break my initial resolution: to write every note of each piece within the month in question. And here is the result – a journey through all twelve months of one year – a trip once around the sun.

From the beginning I found myself taking inspiration for each piece from a particular experience I had each month that seemed to me to encapsulate the mood of the season. *A yellow disc rising from the sea*, for instance was inspired by a visit my wife Claire, my one-and-a-half-year-old son Maurice and I made to Tate Modern one cold foggy morning early in January to see Olafur Eliason's amazing installation, *The Weather Project*. The idea behind February's piece came from seeing pack ice flow down the Hudson River in New York. March found me stuck in the studio watching the endless winter rain and dreaming of spring, while a sudden gloriously sunny day in April inspired *the first day of summer* which was predictably then recorded between particularly violent gusts of wind in the most un-summerlike gale imaginable.

Cumulonimbus was named for the endless ranks of clouds that marched over London that May; June's piece was inspired by the transit of Venus across the sun that we were privileged to witness one morning. I wrote July's piece between orchestral sessions in a studio in Prague where we were recording music for the movie version of *The Hitchhiker's Guide to the Galaxy* and called it *murmuration* after the flock of birds Claire and I had seen wheeling around and around in the floodlights above Prague's Baroque spires the previous night. I missed entirely my favourite month, August, as I was chained to the mixing desk the whole time. I enjoyed the fine weather vicariously through phone calls with Claire, who was travelling with Maurice round the north of England visiting friends. I especially liked her account of a day at the beach in Northumberland where the sea mist rolled in but, rather than obscuring the sun, it was illuminated by it, the whole scene bathed in silver light with everyone splashing around in the waves 'like a *cloudpark*', she said. September threw up the companion piece to April, *the last day of summer*, but by October I was really beginning to feel the pressure of the task and thus I named the tenth piece *cerberus* after the tenth labour of Hercules. November's *eleven* (initially written for solo violin) was conceived as an introduction into the restatement of January's music at the start of *polarisation*, the final and longest piece in the set, which brings us full circle, back to the stillness of winter, before speeding off and ending the journey with a bang.

Writing these pieces was a strange, exhilarating, and sometimes terrifying experience. I've found it a very fulfilling task, commemorating every month of a year with a piece of music, and I hope others will enjoy sharing in my musical journey and will get as much satisfaction from listening to these pieces as I did from writing them. I would like to thank Classic FM, and the PRS Foundation for a fantastic opportunity and a great idea!

Joby Talbot, Camberwell, March 2005

Joby Talbot is the first Classic FM composer in residence. His series of twelve commissions was jointly funded by Classic FM and the PRS Foundation for New Music.

Layout by Fresh Lemon.
Original CD design by Bluw.

CH69718
ISBN 1-84609-159-4

© 2005 Chester Music Limited

Published in Great Britain by Chester Music Limited
Part of the Music Sales Group

Head Office:
8/9 Frith Street, London W1D 3JB, England

Tel +44 (0)20 7434 0066
Fax +44 (0)20 7287 6329

Sales and Hire:
Music Sales Distribution Centre,
Newmarket Road, Bury St Edmunds, Suffolk IP33 3YB, England

Tel +44 (0)1284 702600
Fax +44 (0)1284 768301

www.chesternovello.com

1	JANUARY	a yellow disc rising from the sea	2
2	FEBRUARY	the arctic circle	4
3	MARCH	seed capsule	12
4	APRIL	the first day of summer	16
5	MAY	cumulonimbus	26
6	JUNE	transit of venus	34
7	JULY	murmuration	36
8	AUGUST	cloudpark	40
9	SEPTEMBER	the last day of summer	44
10	OCTOBER	cerberus	50
11	NOVEMBER	eleven	56
12	DECEMBER	polarisation	60

JANUARY:
a yellow disc rising from the sea

Joby Talbot

FEBRUARY:
the arctic circle

Joby Talbot

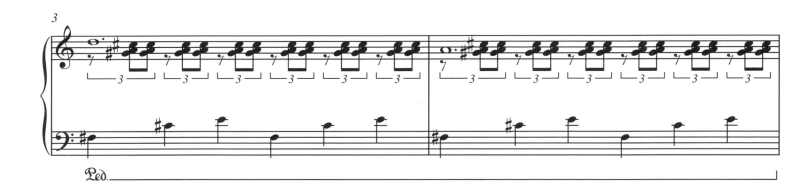

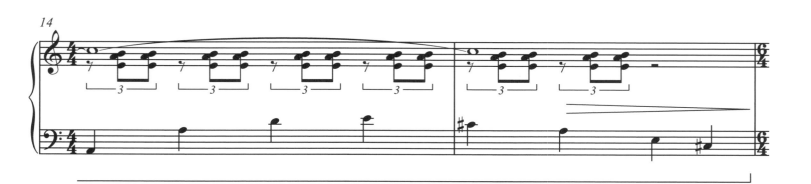

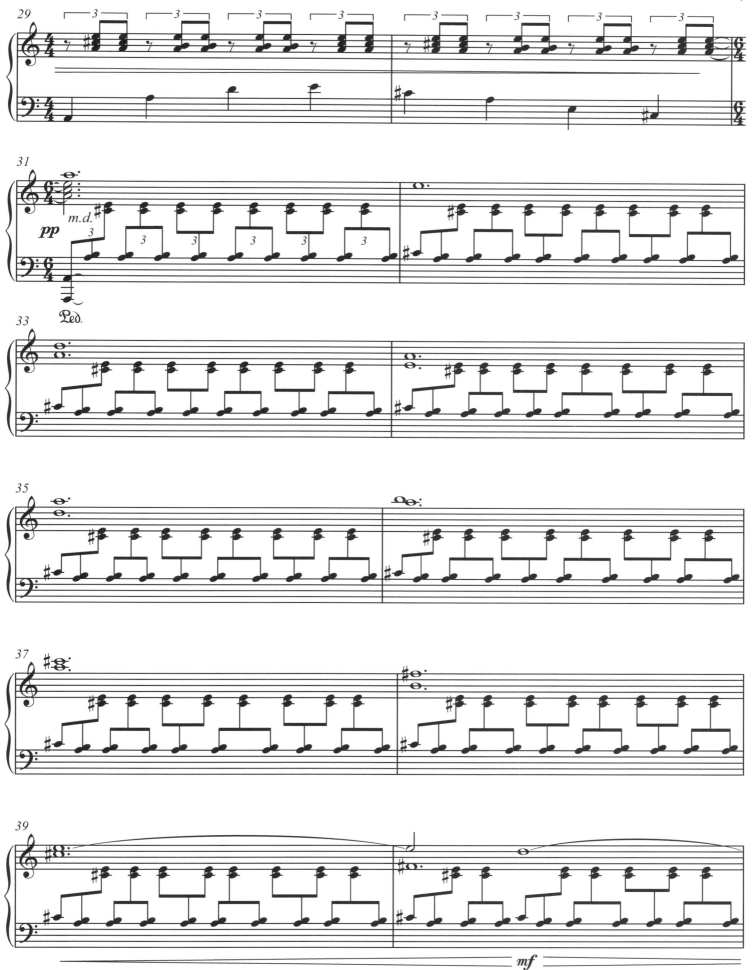

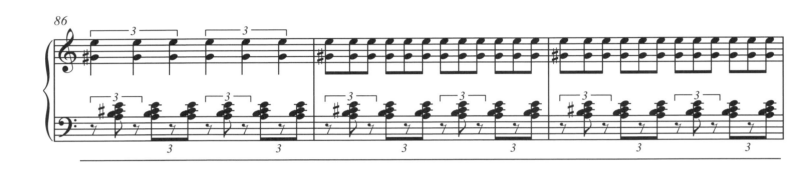

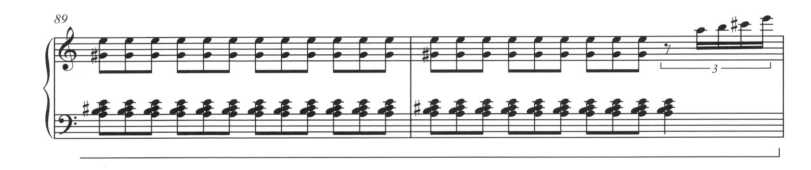

MARCH:
seed capsule

Joby Talbot

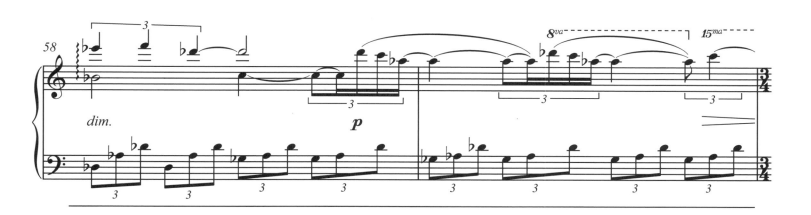

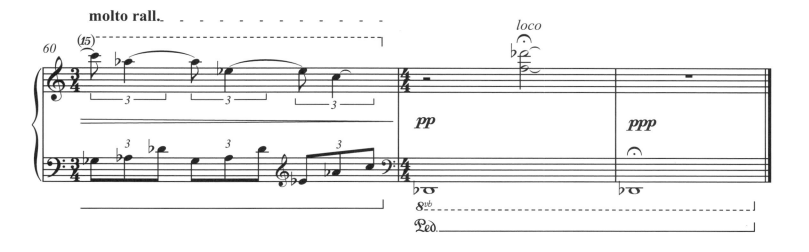

APRIL:
the first day of summer

Joby Talbot

dim. poco a poco

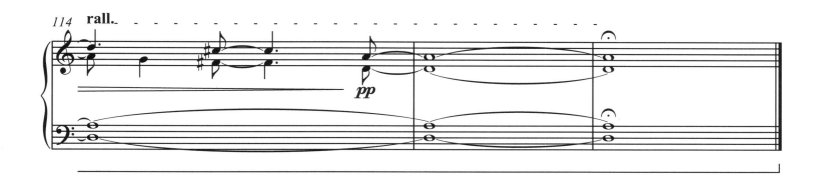

MAY:
cumulonimbus

Joby Talbot

Tempo I

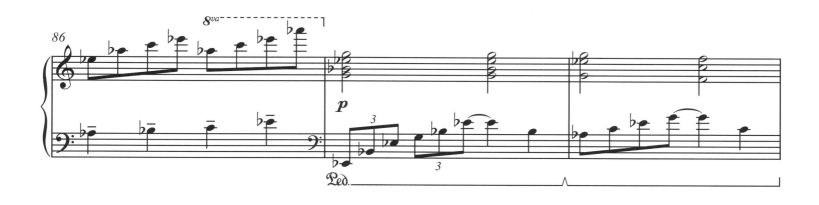

JUNE:
transit of venus

Joby Talbot

JULY:
murmuration

Joby Talbot

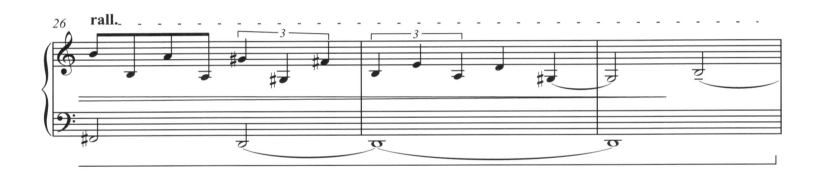

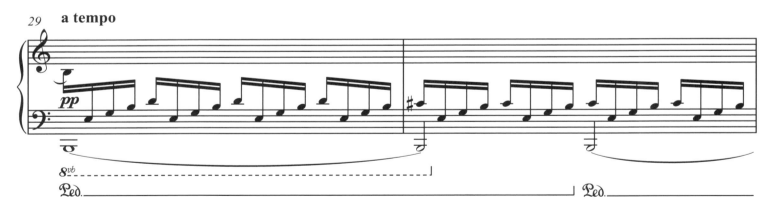

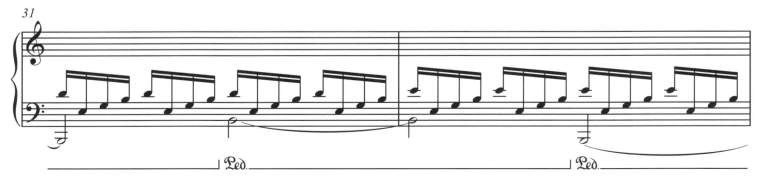

AUGUST:
cloudpark

Joby Talbot

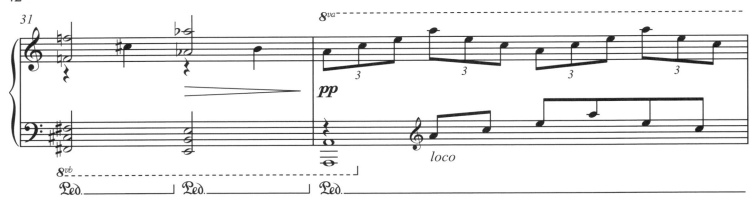

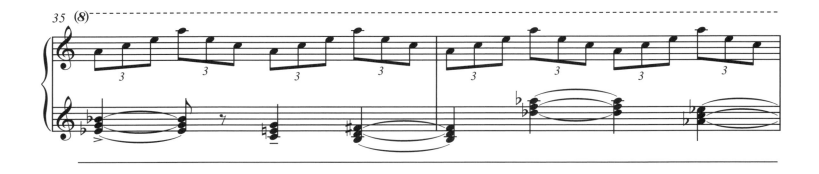

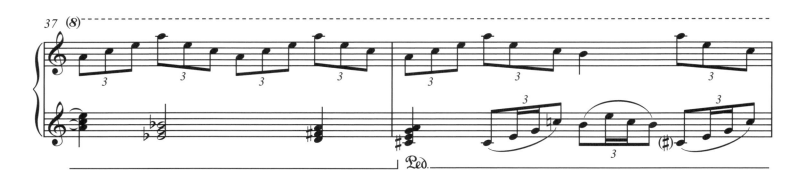

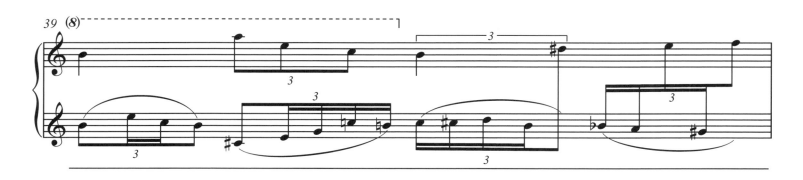

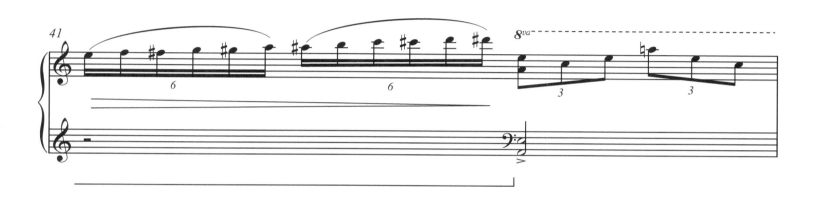

SEPTEMBER:
the last day of summer

Joby Talbot

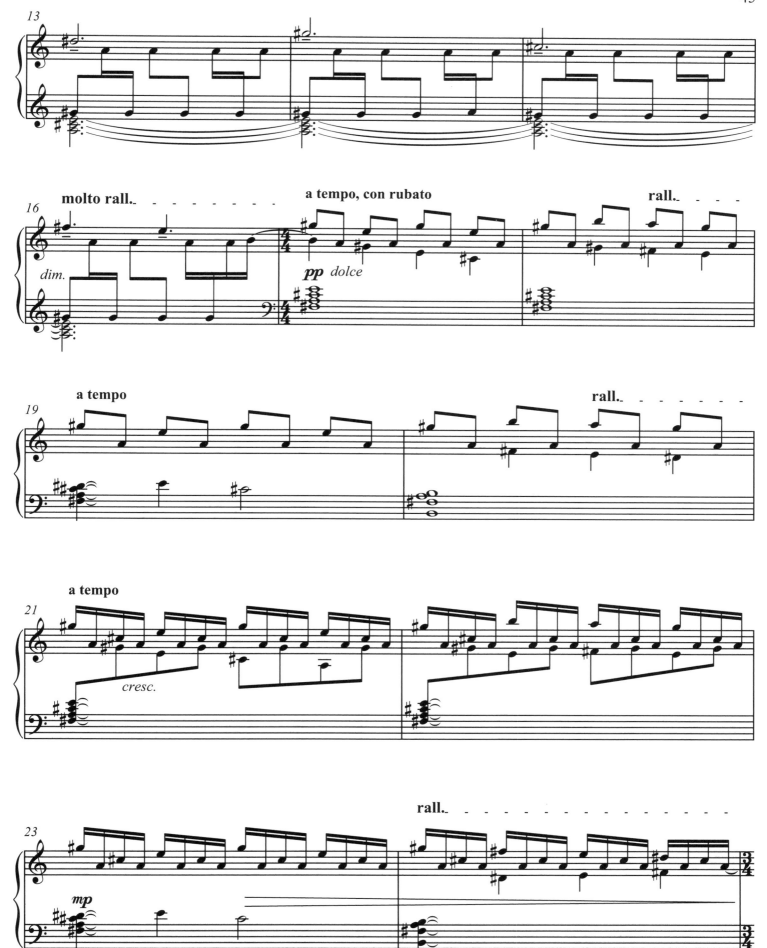

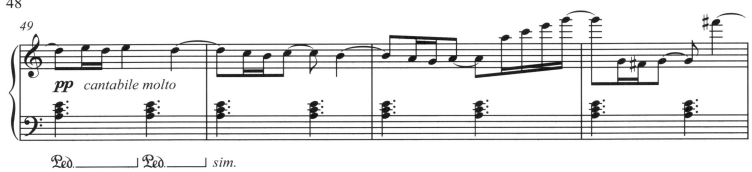

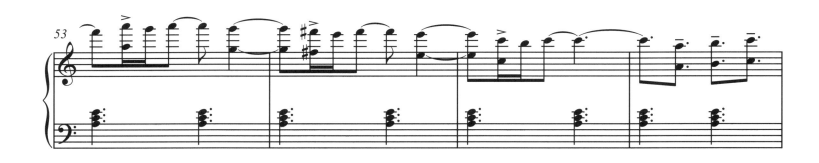

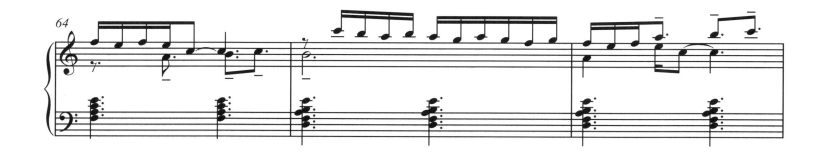

OCTOBER:
cerberus

Joby Talbot

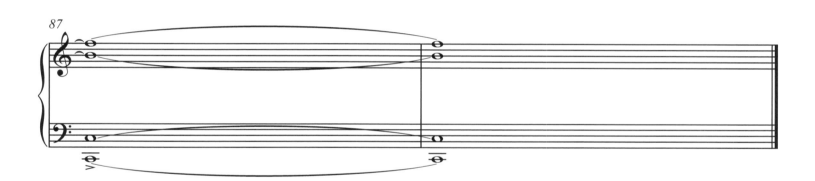

NOVEMBER:
eleven

Joby Talbot

attacca

DECEMBER:
polarisation

Joby Talbot

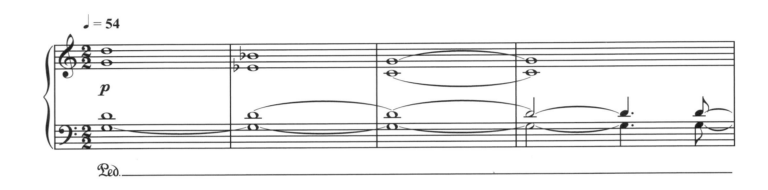

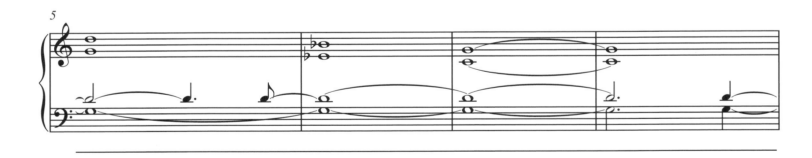

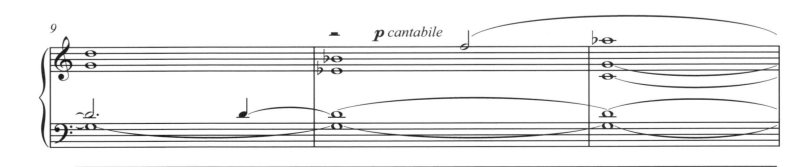

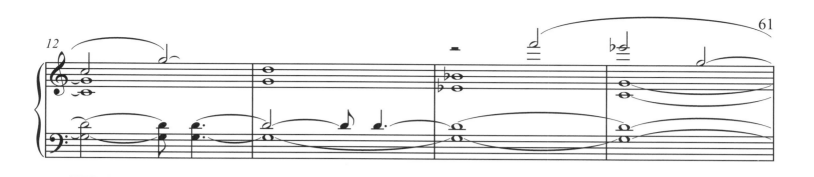

♩ = 108 l'istesso tempo

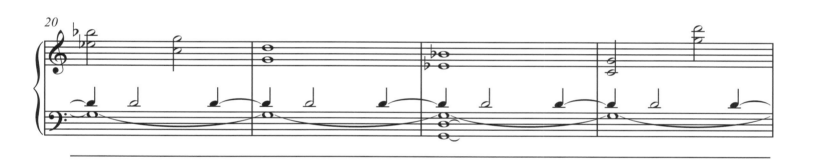

Ped.

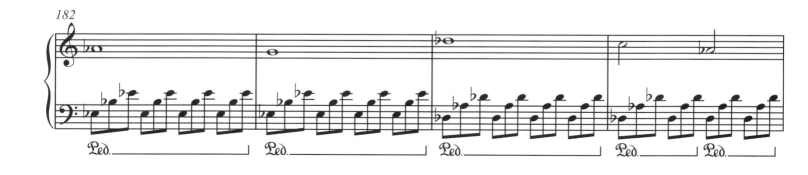

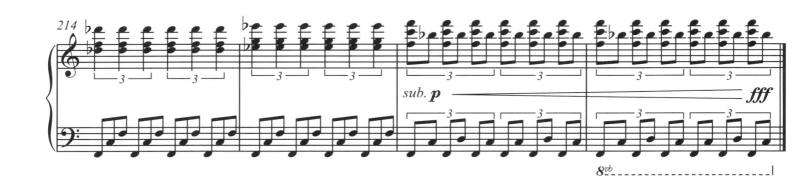